Horsethief Meadows

The Collected Poems of Alex Leavens

edited by

Eric le Fatte and Bruce Parker

Finishing Line Press
Georgetown, Kentucky

Horsethief Meadows

The Collected Poems of Alex Leavens

Copyright © 2023 by The Estate of Alex Leavens
ISBN 979-8-88838-342-1   First Edition
All rights reserved under International and Pan-American Copyright Conventions. No part of this book may be reproduced in any manner whatsoever without written permission from the publisher, except in the case of brief quotations embodied in critical articles and reviews.

This chapbook was made possible in part by donations to the ONE LAST WORD Program. ONE LAST WORD helps to bring the last works of gifted poets to the world.

Publisher: Leah Huete de Maines
FLP Editor: Christen Kincaid
Cover Art: Alex Leavens
Author Photo: The Estate of Alex Leavens
Cover Design: Elizabeth Maines McCleavy

Order online: www.finishinglinepress.com
also available on amazon.com

Author inquiries and mail orders:
Finishing Line Press
P. O. Box 1626
Georgetown, Kentucky 40324
U. S. A.

Table of Contents

Horsethief Meadows 1

The Vulture and the Bear 3

Axe Helve 4

Spring Nettle 5

Pearson Creek 6

Loading a Ship 7

Hive 8

Scappoose Bay 9

Madie DeGraw 10

A Carpenter Bee 11

Refuge on the Metolius 12

On the Stile 13

Tiger Swallowtail 14

The Aspen Grove 15

Four haiku 16

Side Yard Farm 17

Grey Whale Migration 19

The Crows that Live Across the Street from My Mom 20

A Bear's Meadow 21

Winter Wren 22

Black and White Scenes from Today 23

The Red Admiral Butterfly 24

High Lake 25

Dutchman Peak 26

Tracks in Snow 27

The Mountain Lion 28

Three Lynx Creek 29

Workshop 30

Three haiku 32
Cast Lake, Mt. Hood National Forest 33
Moth at the Window 34
Spring in Ellensburg 35
Great Grey Owl 36
The Five Hundred Year-Old Oak 37
Rodin's *The Call to Arms* 38
The Yellow of Tamaracks 39
The Mink 40
The Falconer 41
Sager Axe, Stamped 1928 42
Lower Twin Lake 43
The Birds in My Camp 44
To Build a Fire in the Dark 45
Star Gulch Road 47
Saw-Whet Owl 48

Acknowledgements 49
Biography 51

Foreword

I first met Alex Leavens and encountered his poetry as a participant and host of Portland Ars Poetica, a workshop organized and directed by John Miller, which, after meetings in a local coffee house and then at John's apartment, ultimately found its final meeting place in my home. Alex was warm and friendly, and always brought something good that he had baked for our break halfway through each session. In poem after poem over three years of twice-monthly workshops, Alex took me into wild country that he knew well, where I could walk in his footsteps and see wildlife and the natural surroundings as he saw them, in sharp detail, the colors, sounds, and odors vividly portrayed. On more than one occasion Alex brought a poem that in my view needed no further revision, but was publishable as it was, and I would tell him so on the copy I returned to him along with the others in the group—and publish them he did, and many more besides. Alex took me into his country, and enlarged and enhanced my view of the world. His poetry will take you there, too.

Bruce Parker

Horsethief Meadows

That night in the meadows could read
like the memoir of a snake:
I was warm, suddenly I was cold, and
I didn't know how long the night would last.

And those meadows were more thicket and swamp,
and I didn't want to but I slept on a game trail,
because everywhere else was wet,
and even in my warmest hunting clothes, I shivered
just as the sun went down.

Some reptiles shiver,
and like a snake's body is
its path through life,
mine became a path through the cold;
lying by the stream with a skin of water
over a foot of yellow mud, the sedges
parted at my feet. Knees pressed together,
my hips, spine, and the ribs in my back
found a narrow lane
through the rocks on the ground.

The cold governs half of everything
and it's strange that a snake can survive
without any warmth of its own.
I wasn't cold enough to die, but enough
to be afraid.
On a night like that
it won't matter if your eyes are open or closed.
My imagination escaped to the rumors of wolves,
the cougar-kill downstream.

But I did sleep. I dreamt of a black and white deer
that jumped in and out of a fire.
He took smoldering leaves to eat,
licked the earth to cool his tongue,
and rubbed his burning antlers on the trees.

That's when the owl woke me.
I shivered at the center of the bog,
at the center of her call.
An owl might like to eat a snake
and I was willing to let the cold change me.
It was almost dawn. I would lie still and wait
for the earth to turn
for the sun to warm me.

The Vulture and the Bear

I spooked a vulture off the forest floor.
Her wings pushed the smell
of carrion toward me
and forced a cloud
of blond fur into the air.

Half-buried next to a tree,
I saw a calf and a dog—both
dead as their stench.

Then I heard the curious squeaks,
craned my head around the trunk,
clinging to the tree,
a small bear craned back
just above where the vulture had been.
I watched as he climbed as high as he could,
a yearling boar, he would have
denned with his mother last winter.

I don't blame the first peoples
for believing in shape-shifters.
I have followed one beast through the thicket
only to find another in its place.

I don't blame them for wrapping a blanket
around the night, pricking it with pins
and giving birth to stars.
People have always found comfort in story.

In bear country, I don't blame the rancher
for dumping livestock far from his pasture.
and I understand that bear,
his first summer alone,
why he climbed high into a tree,
to comfort in what his mother taught.

Axe Helve

After an evening's work,
the hoof is cut crooked and bruised
with a purple blood-knot.

It's not clever work
but the craftsmanship is honest and flawed.
The belly doesn't quite swell,
deep cuts won't be sanded out, and
misuse of the farrier's rasp
has burnished my hands hot.

Nothing is perfect,
but I found something
in the looping topography of veins,
in the smoothness of the grain.
I run my hand along the back
and nurse out the hum of a seashell.

It's a good axe helve—
a third of a stave of yew,
honey-red, hard as glass,
too short for a bow.

Stood prized on the workbench,
on its bruised foot,
handle fixed into the axe-eye,
fitting for that old, pitted Hudson Bay;
the bit draws down like the sharp of a beak,
like some little beast, maybe a hawk,
the type of hawk that will visit violence
back on his own kind.

Spring Nettle

It sounded like wind
in the trees
but it was hail
mauling down.

On my side of the meadow,
under the shade of maples,
a crop of nettle:
slender, tilting,
too shy to entertain the sun.

They kept good company
in buttercup and sorrel,
wore braided,
starlet flowers,
and purple stalks, laced
with glass needles.

A towhee dragged leaves
across bare patches of ground,
while the hailstorm
closed like a curtain
over the meadow.

Pearson Creek

Near Ukiah, Oregon

I found mountain lion tracks in the snow,
with yellow needles and crumbs of ice
stuck to the imprints of the toes and pads.

It climbed a game trail out of the valley
and the cold well where the groundwater
pushed its way out of the soil
in frozen coral blooms.

The woods opened and the tracks diverged
where two cats had walked side-by-side.
One took a wary path under a fallen tree,
the other leapt to perch
where it could look across mountains and fields.

Like chasing after a daydream,
I had to imagine in pieces— the wide paw,
rippling shoulder, long tails for balance
and luxury of expression.

I began to see them,
the mother lion, her adolescent cub.
I followed along
as they walked the low edge of the summit,
then slipped back into the valley
with all the behaviors and talents of the cold.

Loading a Ship

> *Cyrus Fulton, oil on canvas, ca.1935*
> *Portland Art Museum Collection*

There's no danger to the longshoremen,
though they stand in shadow on the empty barge,
under the last bundle of wood hoisting onto the ship.

The force from an old tugboat is no threat—
grey smoke sinking off the stack—
but is meant to roil the surface of the water
and make landings
for the reds, greens, hard and soft blues.

The sun shines on the hull of the ship,
where it's brightest, color in soft glare,
where light meets resistance,
it mottles through
salt, parchment, flamingo and rose,
follows lines of rust, lines of age.

Nothing special about the day,
the figures, or the clouds along the Columbia—
it's a red boat and the water is blue,
but a source of light,
with countless surfaces to work upon,
perplexes the superficial,
frames the exterior in warm detail—
this sun's promontory,
this moment's vessel.

Hive

I didn't think
a twenty-year-old memory
would hurt them,
but Chloe climbed
over the same log.
It was the same hive,
the same swarm,
the same screams.

Scappoose Bay

Clouds
stand above the island
like grim walls.

Eagles perch
on either side of the canal
like gargoyles: one, corroded-black,
the other, its white head and tail
ditched with streaks of grey,
as though underneath its feathers
there is stone.

The oaks have not bloomed
and some stand on still-life roots,
where the soil has washed away from the shore—

and some, completely hollowed,
still hold out bare hands
to the sky.

In the shallows,
a carp with gold fins and grey body
writhes in the grasp
of dead limbs
that reach into the channel.

I nose the kayak
further down the canal,
as a heron spans its wings
in the tall grass,

and a yellow iris blooms
out through the water.

Madie DeGraw

The only scars are on the aspen tree. It happened before my time, but I can tell it like I was there—Madie DeGraw and the bear that took her in the middle of the night. She came into the wickiup, and pulled Madie out over two people, but no one heard a thing until the screams—one second she was warm, the next she was cold. But the bear never hurt her, just slipped off the sleeping bag and sniffed her, down there. But the bear couldn't have her, stood on her hind legs and tore into the aspen tree when the young man came into the dark and rain in his underwear to scare it away. Some legends say that a bear who can't have cubs will fall in love with a woman during her moon. That winter, a hunter shot an uncommonly large sow in those same hills. I've known mountain men who could string a few stories together and come up with a tall tale but I believe most of this one. I don't know how long that old aspen tree will be there to hold up the only proof. After too long, who'll be left to say that it had anything to do with love?

A Carpenter Bee

caught a
yellow jacket
midair.

They tumbled
in cursive
to the ground,

where the ant
dragged them in a circle
by a wing.

The bee got away
but the yellow jacket
tucked his head,

and left his vespers
traced in dust.

Refuge on the Metolius

Over a low bridge
and a snow-melt stream,
thirty head of elk went noiseless
over the floor.
Rusty manes and bronze fleece
cut past black-barked pines.
I myself walked quietly
on mats of copper needles.
The only sounds in the after-rain
were droplets from the pine.

It began to snow
as I walked back over
that low bridge. The silver gale
wove flakes through
the fingers of a willow,
sculpted in the reds
of late winter,
all in those tarnished forest colors,
all in that tintype light.

On the Stile

Winslow Homer, 1878

Tom led Caroline across the stile. Her blouse and ribbon took some blue from the hills and that same blue was on the fence boards as her eyes adjusted to the shade. She took care in her good shoes on the tall steps.

Their hands passed over the ridge of the fence like a knot in a rope and they tugged against each other as she took the top step after him. His hands were already rough from woodwork and once she'd seen him bend a tenpenny nail. A memory came to her. She remembered the coast when their mother was pregnant with Tom. She remembered the sand, cold, and pouring it into their father's wide hands and the expanse settled under the sky.

Caroline looked out to the foothills, now rolling under the haze—the mirage of afternoon. "Oh, Thomas," she said, "do you see all that blue? That's what the ocean looks like."

Tiger Swallowtail

It was a gift
to someone new
to butterflies,
who has trouble
convincing them
to hold still—
the tiger swallowtail,
dead, her dull yellow
impaled on the dry grass.
I pried her loose with a twig
and held her in my palm.

A breeze lifted her
back into her lightness
to sail and batter in and out of the shade,
but only lightness,
no life, she fell like paper ash,
slow enough to catch midair,
where I held her in both hands,
shielded her like a match
and broke her hind wing with the slightest touch.

I thought that I should look at her more softly, too—
her wing border, attached with loose embroidery;
the tiger stripes, calligraphy on aging paper,
bold then trailing off,
one as long as the tear down her wing.

I had the sense that I should look at her
more gently
and I had second thoughts
about sliding a pin through her back
and keeping her for display.

The Aspen Grove

I sat down where the wind cornered me
in the tail of an aspen grove
and set my bow where a badger
had mounded old river sand.

Each young tree was bent by antlers,
each tree of good size,
scribbled with claw marks
of climbing bears.

High in the boughs, the wind
articulate in every leaf,
from gust to gust,
the rush and the quiet—
another voice of the forum
in the soft, white bark:

and the wind
found its way down
into the dry mouth of the badger's sett,
down into the earth
to remind the grove
to stay joined
at the root,
to speak as one living thing.

Four haiku

summer evening
a hand from the apartment window
pruning marigolds

Cow Parsnip flowers crowd
to hide the numbers
of their country mailbox.

wet side of the gorge
surprise gift
scorpion in my pocket

I lie down.
Orion turns around the sky.
Venus sleeps above the pines.

Side Yard Farm

Cully Neighborhood, Portland, Oregon

The hens, shooed off the chives,
followed you, while you scraped
mulch from our wheelbarrows
with bare hands.
You spread it in the walkways, fingers raw,
and covered with needles and wood chips.
You sifted through the mixture,
felt for worms as you went along,
picked them out, and buried them like seeds
in the planting soil.

We spoke only through our bodies,
you crouching, scooping,
waiting for me to stumble backward with my barrow.
Hand in the air, you refused my gloves,
with a wrist, brushed back your hair
to watch a mob of crows chase an eagle across the farm.
A dead crow in her grasp,
she flew the length of the black-earth rows,
talons tight around the corpse like a bundle tied in cord—
crows suspended around her,
circling and diving, a carousel of black glass.

Crows, the birds that steal,
had all the farmworkers staring—
their bristled voices bound us all in rope.
I stared, balanced against the weight
of my wheelbarrow,
my boots deep in the mud.

They flew south into the trees
and I don't know how it ended.
I watched the faces turn eastward,
but before a word passed,
you rose, and left before anyone else.

So, I knelt in your place,
plucked worms from the ruts,
and sowed them in beds.
I waited too long to ask your name,
but settled into your futile rescues,
as the chickens scratched along behind me,
and haggled over worms.

Grey Whale Migration

I stepped down from clouds
to stare off a cliff
over a bay full of whales,
over the tide of their breathing.

They heave out of water,
take in the salt air,
fins glance off sunlight.
They roll, crash,
and vanish in mist.

One perch below, a rock seems to move
and the falcon's eye looks into mine.
One black stone eye
before she falls
into the sky above the sea.

I watch her,
like some uncarved witness
high on a cliff matted in salt,
both feet moored to the ground,
a falcon's hook in my skin.

The Crows that Live Across the Street from My Mom

The crow pushed a Cooper's hawk from the trees, where limbs of a horse-chestnut and a maple reached out to one another, where sunlight teetered on the leaves, stumbled through the different shades of green, and both birds fell hard onto the pavement. I'd never seen this type of hawk next to a crow. It looked too small. Its grey wings, long tail, too thin—maybe it was the smaller cousin, the Sharp-Shin. The hawk flew to a branch, lowered its head, and beat out a series of calls. I heard a fledgling crow in the trees and it all seemed fair, whatever counts as fair in the lives of birds. I've seen an eagle snatch a crow off its branch. A mob of crows can kill a hawk or eagle. My friends ate a Redtail that was killed by crows, with instant mashed potatoes, for the best Thanksgiving they ever had. Crows rob each other's nests but they won't forget those who come after their young. They kept an eye on my mom, all the while spoiling her birdbath with food scraps and bones. They attacked her in the open after she saved a fledgling that had fallen in the road, and then for three days as it wandered the sidewalks. So, she kept her distance and followed wherever it wanted to go, but kept a lookout for cars, like she used to do for her children and her grandchildren when we were young.

A Bear's Meadow

There's a new trail across the meadow
where all the bears share muddy tracks
that won't heal over.
It's been two springs since I've been here
and the snowmelt pond has already dried.

Dark, stunted reeds show through the softer green
as a breeze stirs in the grass
and all the butterflies rise up together
then land to redraw the pattern of flowers.

A young bear has come along that same path
to feed on the spring grasses.
She steps just far enough into the clearing
for the sunlight to bristle her long fur.

There is little wind, now, but she lifts her thin muzzle
and knows someone is there.
She pivots on tip-toe and is quickly dissembled
in the patchwork of the forest.

All around the meadow, the evening sun
wraps every long needle in the pines
and the white stalk of an old spruce
shows through its boughs.

Before the sun goes down
another bear comes,
with scars across his face
and missing patches of fur.
A massive bear, the kind to leave permanent tracks
on the earth.

He walks well into the meadow
and raises his snout. His head drifts side-to-side
before he turns, swaying back and forth
on the stiffness in his legs,
to slowly retrace his steps.

Winter Wren

Winter had set
but there were still
spiders on the snow
for the wren who landed
in the last cave of green
under a log.

No matter how much
I wanted him to,
he would not sing.

But knowing him,
knowing his song,
I looked up the mountainside,
up the columns of white
on every trunk,
into the wind
that turned tree tops
and filled the canopy
with running furls of snow.

I looked back down
and he was gone;
somewhere still nearby
hunting spiders.

Black and White Scenes from Today

I.

patches of moss
      landless urchins
   sail away
         from the maple

        a band of crows
           greedy for insects
tears the open-work
        of dark gauze

no crow sings
     drifts in the debris
        falls by one
           by two

this winter wind
      washes them away

II.

Robins and sparrows don't like the waxwings, the bands that swing through town tied together with delighted noise, trapeze together through bare branches for every last ornamental fruit. Then they're gone. They've taken away everything that was there and everything they brought, bright yellow tail-bands, red-polish tips of wings. It's a problem for the local birds when winter goes on this long. There are too many. They seem too happy.

The Red Admiral Butterfly

She sunned her wings in a spotlight,
without entitled airs.
She'll keep to the thicket all summer long, close to the forest floor,
the curly dock and nettles where she lays her eggs.

She's drawn to her own colors
but wouldn't come to the tiger lily I picked—all I had to offer.
Her wings beat slow like a bellows,
black, coal-red, spots of ash,
she was the last remains of a fire,

where the late-day sun had broken through,
where the shadows of leaves closed in—
all the nicks and tears in the cloth of her wings,
and once summer's gone, she'll burn out again.

She lifted off, circled around me faster than I could turn my head.
I haven't seen her again, though I take the trail more often now,
and take it just for her.

High Lake

Fish Creek Mt., Oregon

I look for the wind,
find its brush strokes
on the surface of the lake,
follow it to the terrace of grey,
inlaid boulder to the cliffs—
not grand, but sheer and guarded.
I could stand back,
cup the entire body of water
in two big handfuls,
like this little mountain holds it
on this narrow shelf.
It slips through our fingers,
down steep channels
into trees.

I turn
look to where Mt. Hood
spreads its mantle
across a greater wilderness—
equal to the horizon,
equal to the morning sun.

Dutchman Peak

The curiosity on his face could have been mistaken for affection—the way he looked at me from under his round-toy ears, brown silk fur down to the ground and sunlight in pieces all around him. I had seen his tracks over and over, the soft mold of his prints, scars of his claws in the mud. In the deep snow he walked in my tracks as a matter of ease, and I left superstition alone and walked in his. He wasn't on the far side of Dutchman Peak, in the sun and spring grass where I see all my bears. Feet still tender, he stayed close to the den, there on the north side where he tore into every stump and downed log. He might be happy enough out of the sun, happy enough to root for bees and grubs and eat and eat all day long like we want and want, but we're still unhappy. We met in the evening, when color was left to my imagination, when meadows blushed back at the sun, the spruces light blue, and he was brown as a chestnut.

Tracks in Snow

Christmas Eve 2019

A cougar had wandered
down the streambed.
The warmth of her paws
fused the snow into ice
and her tracks erased
the hoofprints of the deer she followed.

Some narrow hooves still appeared
in the new snow that quieted the valley,
and left no space for shadows
under the trees.

I've found signs there all year—
all the wildlife that's passed through that hollow,
like through the narrow of an hourglass.

The Mountain Lion

Through the smoke of wildfires,
the mountain lion had the same tint as the moon—
dark copper, as well as I could see
through the haze that burned my eyes,
what, at first I thought was a deer,
but too low to the ground,
and its body, a different kind of mass:
tendon and muscle at work under the skin,
the visible strength,
his vessel and passenger.
Where the smog held low to the valley
he climbed
the zig-zag of a deer trail
like flames climb
into tree tops
to ferry substances
no longer bound to earth,
which still require
a path to be set free.

Three Lynx Creek

Camp is an old logging skid
under second growth.
Winter stars
show through the canopy.

The soil mends
under patches
of hearts of ginger leaves,
under kingdoms
of white mushrooms.

We lie on our backs
by a mount of coals
that we measure against
the circumference of the world

and I reach a hand
into the lucid cold,
to the stars:
the crop of night trees
that long to fall
and be gathered.

Workshop

Jaws from a heavy set of pliers
reach out from the plumbing bag.
The basement floor is a rookery
of toolboxes and bags, and white paint buckets
full of wood chisels and work lamps and drill motors,

more white buckets with concrete and leveler dried on the rims
and full of more tools, and clear plastic jam jars:
egglets for pan-head, drywall, and many other types of screws.

A narrow path winds to the workbench
through the buckets and bags
and coiled, orange-black cords.
In the little space there is to work
is the sewing box I've made
for the wife of a friend; for the thread, the yarn,
her wooden darning egg shaped like a mushroom.

It's not a nice box. I built it as a hollow block
then cut off the lid on the table saw.
Quarter-inch plywood nailed and stained,
I've only added glue as an after-thought—
in the open seams where gravity should still operate
but the glue stays out in globes;
I coax it down with the point of a nail.

I make boxes without handles or furniture that shows.
I prefer the simplest shape,
and the shapes in the clouds in the grain.
There's a rifle box down here somewhere—
slats of alder catch you in one long draw of the eye.
The one from an oak pallet sits upstairs,
weathered and stained, it matches the grey and red
of the stuffed kestrel perched by its side.

The sewing box, that looks something like a building block,
the stain has found its way into the plywood,
into the striations and the clouds.

Tools leak out of the walls.
They hang from hooks,
and pour out from the shelves: mill file, compressor hose,
flat bar and cat's paw.
A four-foot pipe wrench hangs head down,
the tired end of a long, steel taper;
a fossil or a sculpture with worn out jaws.

Circular sawblades bunch on a nail,
discarded clock-faces;
arrangements of teeth,
wherever they happened
to stop spinning in time.

She wants to have a box on the floor
by her sitting pillow and the low table;
for her sewing and her darning,
a simple box in the empty corner.

There's sawdust in the apron threads and the coffee.
I'll stay down here a little longer, like I always do,
after the air has been bitten—the sting of wood vapor,
hammer blows, the final ring of the saw; down here,
where teeth have many minutes for the hour.

Three haiku

rusty barbed wire
looms for cottonwood down
for the spider's thread

Three gravel mountains
on the barge,
stand-ins for St Helens.

The falcon, a copper stain
where the steel made an X
under the bridge.

Cast Lake, Mt. Hood National Forest

the long note of a thrush
thin like an awl across the lake

no sunshine or blue sky
only dark trees reflected on the water

the lake is ringed
with silver-white alders

new leaves from red sprouts
blocks of snow patch frozen mud

the forest passes
through the lake

as something more
in the parentheses of ripples

something painted over
that shows through from underneath

in those loose flashes
it touches the unconscious

then is quietly fixed
as it is

the remains of winter
on the fickle surface

palette of spring
fastened to the stillness below

Moth at the Window

Portland during the forest fires, September 2017

Sunlight spread evenly through the glass
and the moth battered herself against the window to get out.
There was a stained-glass train leaning on the sill,
its red banners trailing.

She landed on the puffs of yellow smoke trapped in circles of lead,
rising from the stack,
then lighted on the coal car, obsidian black,
the faintest sunlight running through.

Her wings: stone-linen, black line, scalloped on the fringe.
She seemed separate from her own colors
and wore them like slips applied to clay.

No light passed through her wings,
but even in her stillness,
she kept to her chase
toward the brightest point in the sky.

I dried the inside of a green tumbler
and caught her against my palm
and the room where I held her seemed a larger cage.
When I opened the window to set her free,
ash and smoke blew in.
I shut it quickly to keep her outside
and watched her land on a maple
tinted with auburn and red.

Spring in Ellensburg

Three new bricks,
dusting of soot:

walls to withstand
all four seasons.

Great Grey Owl

I didn't hear the owl
land in the pine.
I saw the shadow of her wings
spread across the meadow
with the long shadows of trees.

She stood with the sun behind her
shining through the unkempt
feathers at her feet.

She never stopped moving
or circling her head
and I wondered what she saw
that made her drop to the ground
so often for nothing.

She caught herself from falling
more than she flew:
heavy, soundless,
tail, wing,
all her feathers open
underneath.

There had been a rumor of her
but the squirrels had stopped calling.
Now she flew in the open at dusk,
no echo of flight against the ground
no beat of air underneath.

The Five Hundred Year-Old Oak

The limbs, trees unto themselves;
as many broken as whole,
as many that touch ground
as reach out high.

In sleeves of moss and licorice fern
they rest in neighboring oaks,
in the crooks of alders.
They spider and twist
and creep through tall grass

at the edge of the grove and the field
where the heron patiently collects frogs,
where there are hawks
with tails to match willow and dogwood,

and today, for five hundred years,
the harrier quick-turns in her flight,
then lands to rest
until the wind
picks her back up
again.

Rodin's *The Call to Arms*

How does the angel
suffer the broken wing?
She laments all we've lost,
yet cries out for war.

Given as bronze
her feathers seem stone.
She ascends despite her injury
and the weight of the soldier—

he leans into her,
wounded, one hand still
on the hilt of his sword.

They are one figure.
She is his agony
rising.

The Yellow of Tamaracks

Hidden behind fir and pine,
their color flashes,
and for a moment
I think it's the sun,
the only sun
under ten days of grey and snow;

not a promise but a memory
of a season I lost at sunset,
when sunlight, squandered on mountain dust,
set the buttes in gold
and the pine held their boughs like beggars.

Summer turned to winter while I slept.
I woke in the early morning,
wind and clouds and snow pressing
over my Blue Mountains.

That sun was shining
on the ground
in minced rays
where yellow needles had fallen

on the snow, where I found the tracks
of a bull elk, a bear,
a mountain lion,
all together on a narrow path.

The Mink

I saw that mink again
when I got to the lake.
In the water she always looks
much larger, but on land
she's a thin, wet brush.
She made her way back and forth
across the logs to the thicket,
but what she took to cache was too small to see;
once I caught a hint of dark shell.

I see her at that lake nobody knows—
her private afternoons fishing and chasing ducks
and I could get bored
watching so long
but I'm fond of restless creatures
so at home off solid ground.

She swam the length of the shallows
in a sequence of somersaults
and the ripples broke shadows of fir trees
and the reflections of willow.
She has a talent for diving into the cloudy water
after the invisible things
she desires.
She runs away with them
out in the open.

The Falconer

I saw him
before the rain,
guiding his falcon
in the rail yard.

He swung a scrap of fur
on the end of a rope.

Between the fuel tanks
and boxcars,
I saw grey wings,
a rusty tail.

He swung the rope
like a bull roarer,
as if to call in
the friends of his tribe
from long ago,
when they would have gathered
in ceremony
to bait the wind
and storm.

Sager Axe, Stamped 1928

Centralia, Washington

I wanted to buy that Sager axe,
the brand of its day,
an old double-bit, dimpled on the cheek
where it served as a hammer to drive wedges.

It was a Puget Sound pattern with narrow blades,
made to sink deep into mammoth cedars,
but not the right axe for splitting rounds.

It needed a handle, oil, and nicks
filed out of the blade,
but I don't fix axes anymore.

Could have bought it
and that old grindstone,
and I imagined a new helve
for the axe, a hand-crank
and wooden stand for the stone.

But I left them both in the rust-bin
with tools not half their worth,
with no idea of the work they would do,
just what I would put into their care.

I'm not fixing tools these days—
but I've found that a tool's more honest
after it's been used—it shows the hand
of the one who owned it.

Lower Twin Lake

Mt. Hood National Forest

The wind curves my fishing line
where it lies on the water,
bows the band of sunlight
that reaches across the lake to me.

Trees black,
backlit by the sun,
the wind brings clouds
over their serrated tines,
and the evening too early.
The wind that sometimes speaks for ghosts
inks the sun away and gossips through the leaves,
scribbles messages across the water,
then is gone,
and the sun-haze gone,
trees evergreen again,
white snags teething on the bank.

Underwater,
the silver spinner comes back
over and over, alone.
The water stays warm,
wills to have me longer,
wraps loosely around my legs.

I have to stay,
spread my toes
wider in the mud,
wade further in.

The Birds in My Camp

Her fledgling nearby,
the raven circles twice,
twice daily.

Red tanager,
bright moment
through clouds of stone.

Mountain chickadee
wobbles off the pine cone,
brushes the dust.

The flicker outruns
the sharp-shin—
needle slips the thread.

The vireo wrestles astounding facts.
Why yes. Why no.
Why yes. Why no.

New, faraway voice,
the Stellar's jay, I learn,
after I've come home.

To Build a Fire in the Dark

I felt my way back
to the shelter
made of boughs
to the bed
made of leaves.

Through the cold
I felt
for the bow
and hearth board

held blind
to the form
to spin the wooden drill
till the ember
took shape

to glow by the toes
of my bare foot—
a small practical matter
and its place
in the center of the dark.

To rest
half-buried in the leaves
warmed by the fire
that blew out
with a barred owl's call

still glowed
as coals
crystallized in red
the echo
on the skins of the trees

still held its place
that small matter

of living
at the center
of the dark.

Star Gulch Road

There was nothing for me in the hills,
in the last basins of November light,
in the yellow oaks and mountain mahogany,
and there were no acorns for the bears.

But down on Star Gulch Road there was a screech owl
by the warning sign of a gold claim
squinting under its feather horns.
It sat in the road all day
and flew just out of reach of cars.

In the hills, there was nothing but last year's bear scat—
red pearls of undigested berries,
and no reason to look over my shoulder.

You can usually hear bears coming,
but the ones I see just appear:
at the meadow last spring,
she announced herself quietly, stepped from the trees
pigeon-toed and roaming black.

She stood on the hillock by the stump
where the owl landed the year before
and stayed for an evening,
and from that small eminence,
looked my way.

On my way back to camp
I saw the screech owl
lying in the ditch on its side.
I don't know where owls go when they die.

Some stories say that bears come from the stars
and go back when they die. I like to think
that's where they go when they sleep all winter,
that, dreaming, they wander the hills of someplace far away,
and that it's always summer for a bear.

Saw-Whet Owl

The best I could see in the dark,
shapes of wings broke free
from the other night shapes,
and flew low,
across the snowy ground.

When I found the owl
under the hemlock
his yellow eyes sharpened
under the flashlight.

He's like me. Small.
He might not make it through winter.
But he is well-suited for the night,
and fierce, given his size.

He had just enough strength,
just enough eyesight,
just enough quiet on the wing.

He's just shrewd enough with the talon
to lever over his prey.

Acknowledgements

Grateful acknowledgment is made to the editors and staffs of the following publications in which these poems first appeared.

Frogpond haiku beginning "summer evening"

CIRQUE "Dutchman Peak", "The Vulture and the Bear", "Maddie DeGraw", "The Crows that Live Across the Street from My Mom"

Clover "Loading a Ship", "Axe Helve"

Montana Mouthful "High Lake"

Perceptions "Hive", "Side Yard Farm", "Rodin's *The Call to Arms*", "Cast Lake, Mt. Hood National Forest", "Horsethief Meadows" "Tiger Swallowtail", "Refuge on the Metrolius", "Scappoose Bay"

The Ekphrastic Review "On the Stile"

Tiny Seed Journal "Great Grey Owl", "A Carpenter Bee", "Tracks in Snow", "The Mountain Lion", "The Five Hundred Year-Old Oak", "Grey Whale Migration"

Wild Roof Journal "Scappoose Bay", "Saw-Whet Owl"

Windfall "Moth at the Window", "The Yellow of Tamaracks", "Sager Axe, Stamped 1928", "Lower Twin Lake"

Alex Alan Leavens, was born on July 30, 1975 and raised in Portland, Oregon, as a fourth- generation Oregonian, whose great-grandfather arrived in 1895. He developed his interest in the outdoors as a child, and attended Prescott College in Arizona, where he lived for a year in a wickiup he designed and built. He also attended the Boulder Outdoor Survival School, which led him to start two businesses: the Old Federal Ax Company and the Oregon School of Survival and Tracking. He taught skills ranging from making primitive pottery of the Anasazi tradition to animal track identification. He also served as a firefighter in Arizona, southern California, and the Olympic National Park.

Alex later received a Bachelors degree in English Literature at Portland State University, where he graduated summa cum laude. He honed his craftsmanship skills at properties he and his family owned in Portland, volunteered at the Portland Museum of Art, became an expert baker and charcuterist, and hunted and fished throughout the Oregon backcountry. He also began writing—first a novel, *The Border*, and then poems infused with his devotion to craftsmanship, art, and a unique perspective on nature. In just a few years, Alex published numerous poems in literary magazines, including *Cathexis Northwest, Cirque, Clover, The Ekphrastic Review, Frogpond, Modern Haiku, Montana Mouthful, Tiny Seed Literary Journal, Perceptions Magazine, Wild Roof Journal*, and *Windfall*. Sadly, as his career as a poet began to flourish, Alex Leavens died by suicide on August 13, 2021. The poems he left behind are gathered here.

   —Eric le Fatte

www.ingramcontent.com/pod-product-compliance
Lightning Source LLC
Chambersburg PA
CBHW020343170426
43200CB00006B/484